Bajra Khichdi

ACIDITY COOKBOOK

50 Stomach-Friendly Recipes

S&C
SANJAY & CO.
MUMBAI

First Printing : 2007

ISBN : 978-8-189491-51-2

Price: Rs. 89/-

Published & Distributed by : **Sanjay & Company**

353/A-1, Shah & Nahar Industrial Estate, Dhanraj Mill Compound, Lower Parel (W), Mumbai - 400 013. INDIA.

Tel. : (91-22) 2496 8068 • Fax : (91-22) 2496 5876 • E-mail : sanjay@tarladalal.com

UK and USA customers can call us on :

UK : 02080029533 • USA : 213-634-1406

For books, Membership on **tarladalal.com**, Subscription for **Cooking & More** and Recipe queries

Timing : 9.30 a.m. to 7.00 p.m. (IST), from Monday to Saturday

Local call charges applicable

Recipe Research & Production Design
Arati Fedane

Nutritionists
Nisha Katira
Sapna Kamdar

Typesetting
Adityas Enterprises

Designed by
Satyamangal Rege

Printed by
Minal Sales Agencies, Mumbai.

DISCLAIMER

While every precaution has been taken in the preparation of this book, the publishers and the author assume no responsibility for errors or omissions. Neither is any liability assumed for damages resulting from the use of information contained herein. And of course, no book is a substitute for a qualified medical advice. So it is wiser to modify your dietary patterns under the supervision of a doctor or a nutritionist.

BULK PURCHASES

Tarla Dalal Cookbooks are ideal gifts. If you are interested in buying more than 500 assorted copies of Tarla Dalal Cookbooks at special prices, please contact us at 91-22-2496 8068 or email : sanjay@tarladalal.com

INTRODUCTION

A gift of modern fast-paced life, hurried meals and loads of stress leads to acidity.

Acidity, a common ailment that we all suffer from time to time — that awful burning sensation in the heart or chest. Acidity is caused by excessive secretion of the normal acids in the stomach. But when the secretion is excessive, it causes a burning sensation just below or behind the chest and the stomach.

Wrong eating habits, unhealthy eating pattern, excessive spices, stress etc. are the causes of acidity. Besides this, wrong food choice can be a cause too. For example, there are certain foods that produce acids and some that produce alkali in our body. Eating acidic foods such as pickles, oily foods, chocolates etc. in excessive amounts can aggravate the disorder; hence opting for alkaline foods like *bajra, jowar,* ladies fingers, bananas etc. is the right way to beat acidity naturally.

Instead of popping antacids every now and then, turn to mother nature for natural remedies and cure. My book **"Acidity Cookbook"** is an attempt to do so with a range of 50 healthy recipes that are planned keeping in mind the do's and don'ts for acidity. Aware about the trouble and discomfort that one faces while suffering from acidity, my qualified team of chefs and nutritionist and I have formulated simple recipes that are made using alkaline foods, less spices and are cooked in less oil. Along with this, there are certain foods like onions, kokum, mint etc., which do wonders for acidity, are used in recipes like ***Minty Stuffed Parathas,*** page 51, ***Pyazwali Bhindi,*** page 62, ***Kokum Sherbet,*** page 98, *etc.*

Also included is a comprehensive information on acidity, its causes, symptoms, ways to ease it, list of acidic and alkaline foods and natural remedies for you to know everything about acidity and how to overcome it yourself.

Learn how to eat and live right to combat acidity with a range of delicious and healthy recipes!

Happy cooking!

Tarla Dalal

CONTENTS

What's Acidity?

Acidity is a form of indigestion in which there is accumulation of acid leading to a burning sensation in the stomach and the digestive tract. The stomach periodically produces acid to aid digestion. It is when we don't eat at regular intervals or are excessively stressed the stomach produces more acids which harms our body.

What causes Acidity?

'Hurry, worry and curry', in other words: eating in haste, stress and spicy foods are the primary causes of acidity. Besides these, given below are some of the other causes for acidity.

- Irregular Meals
- Excessive consumption of oily and spicy foods
- Stress
- Over eating especially before going to bed
- Bad posture after meals
- Excessive alcohol consumption

Are you a victim to acidity? Find out here....
Yes, you might be, if you have the following symptoms....

- Burning sensation in the digestive tract
- Headache
- Sour burps
- Dizziness due to hypoglycemia (low blood sugar levels)

Food Guide for Acidity

Listed below is the list of acidic and alkaline foods, which will help to make your food choices very simple. These foods are classified on the basis of their acidic or alkaline nature, however there are certain foods that are acidic in nature but on digestion form alkali in our body and do not cause or aggravate acidity.

So if you suffer from acidity quite often try to avoid or restrict acidic foods (as given in the table below) whereas alkaline foods can be eaten freely. ***Although these foods are classified for you to make wise choices, the reaction of each food is very individualistic and vary from person to person hence pick up foods that suit you the best and help you keep away from acidity.***

Food Groups	**Acidic**	**Alkaline**
Cereals	Cereals like wheat❖, rice❖, dry corn etc and their flour, their products like bread, pasta, noodles, vermicelli, *poha*❖, *rawa*❖, oats❖, brown rice❖, buckwheat○ and ragi (nachni)○.	Jowar and bajra.
Pulses & Legumes	All dals❖ and pulses❖ especially tuvar dal❖, soyabeans❖ and its products like milk, granules, chunks etc., chana dal flour (*besan*) etc.	All sprouts.

Food Groups	Acidic	Alkaline
Milk and milk products	Cheese, paneer, mayonnaise, butter and cream.	Milk❑ (chilled), curds❑, ice creams❑ and milkshakes❑.
Vegetables	Asparagus tips (white) and cooked spinach.	Green leafy vegetables like raw spinach, fenugreek, amaranth etc. lettuce, asparagus greens, cabbage, brinjal, ladies fingers, mushrooms, green peas, cucumber, onions, potatoes, carrots, pumpkin, radish, tomatoes, broccoli etc.
Fruits	Plums, olives, prunes, lemon❖❖, oranges❖❖, pineapple❖❖, sweet limes❖❖, processed fruit juices, canned fruits.	All other fruits like bananas, mangoes, grapes, apples, berries, figs, papaya, peaches, watermelon, chickoo, pear, muskmelon etc.
Nuts and Oilseeds	Dry coconut, walnuts, peanuts, and cashewnuts.	Almonds, dry figs, dry dates, raisins, apricots and fresh coconut.
Miscellaneous	Tea, coffee, alcohol, vinegar, aerated beverages, spicy and fried foods, pickles, chocolate, MSG (Mono Sodium Glutamate), margarine, fermented foods like idlis, dosas, dhoklas etc, confectionary, mithai, sugar, artificial sweeteners, non-veg foods, eggs and other processed foods.	Ginger tea, herbal tea, honey and cinnamon.

❖ These foods are acidic in nature but are an important part of our daily diet and are nutritious too, hence do not avoid them totally. These foods may react differently for each one of us, hence eat them in moderation and combine with other alkaline foods e.g. mix rice (acidic) with lots of vegetables (alkaline), have *chapati* (acidic) with sprouts (alkaline) etc. With time find out which foods, and in what quantity from this category suits your body constitution.

○ This food is difficult to classify as acidic or alkaline hence have it only if it suits you.

❑ These foods are considered to be neutral, however their reactions are individualistic. Hence have them in the amounts that suit you.

❖❖ These fruits are acidic in nature but on digestion they turn alkaline and thus do not cause acidity. However if you already have acidity, its excess consumption may aggravate it, so have them in the amounts that suit you.

Ease your Acidity for NOW and FOREVER

Identifying and avoiding the causative factors are essential in the treatment of acidity. **A suitable diet must be strictly followed avoiding spicy, salty and acidic foods. Plenty of fresh air, exercise, a relaxed mind and the correct foods does wonders to relive acidity. Work on soothing your body and mind for this is just the best way to keep acidity at bay.** Here are a few general guidelines to keep acidity at bay.

- Eat in a calm and stress-free environment. Avoid irregular and hurried meals.
- Regular eating habits and a healthy diet can prevent acidity. Do not remain hungry for a long time and don't overeat at the same time. Both are root cause of acidity.
- Avoid eating outside too frequent as the outside foods.

- Eat small and frequent meals as small amount of food each time would exert less workload on the stomach and therefore release less acid secretion for digestion.
- Have plenty of raw foods, salads and juices. Their alkaline nature helps avoid acidity.
- Too spicy food is sure to cause that burning sensation. So it's better avoided.
- Restrict the consumption of oil to minimal. Avoid fried foods as these foods remain in the stomach longer and hence more acid is secreted for their digestion, which is the cause of acidity.
- Milk, curds and *paneer* (cottage cheese) have an individual effect. To some they are cooling and help overcome acidity whereas some feel they aggravate acidity. So you need to make your choice.
- Restrict the excess consumption of pulses like rajma, moong etc. if they cause gas and then acidity or have them in combination with other alkaline foods like veggies.
- Sprouts, though alkaline can be gas forming for some if consumed in large quantities and usually for dinner (late), hence avoid their consumption if you feel bloated after having them or have them occasionally and during the day.
- Drink plenty of water (at least 6 to 8 glasses per day) and other fluids to maintain the acid balance in the stomach. Have 3 to 4 glasses of buttermilk everyday if you can handle it, as it is said to be 'God's Nectar' a great reliever of acidity.
- Have your evening meals at least two to three hours before going to bed.
- Maintain upright position during and at least 45 minutes after eating each meal to enhance digestion.
- Exercise or meditate at least 15 to 20 minutes in the morning to reduce stress.
- Stop smoking and cut down on alcohol.

Foods that Heal Acidity

Though antacids provide immediate relief of symptoms by neutralizing the excess acid secretion, excessive and frequent consumption of medications can have ill effects on health. Mother nature provides us with number of foods that can work wonders for acidity; here are a few kitchen remedies that are sure to ease your discomfort...

- **Kokum:** Sherbet made with kokum and perked with jeera is excellent in keeping acidity at bay. Check out the recipe of ***Kokum Sherbet,*** page 98.
- **Lemon:** Juice of one lemon mixed in half glass of water and ½ teaspoon sugar if consumed before meals helps to relieve acidity.
- **Vegetable juices:** Juices of vegetables like carrot, cucumber, radish or beetroot help to balance the acid in the stomach due to their alkaline nature. Feel free to add a pinch of salt and pepper to enhance the flavour of these juices.
- **Mint (*phudina*):** Fresh mint juice taken every day or fresh mint leaves boiled in a cup of water and sipped slowly after meals also helps to keep the stomach acids at bay. Turn to ***Minty Stuffed Parathas,*** page 51.
- **Onion (*pyaz*):** The juice of onions is an excellent remedy for acidity. Have them in salads with your meals or alternatively, you can also try a whole wheat flour or jowar rotis made with onions as done in the recipe of ***Jowar Pyaz ki Roti,*** page 48 and ***Bhindi Do Pyaza,*** page 62.

Healthy Brown Onion Soup

Zesty potato balls add flavour to this simple and elegant soup.

Preparation Time: 10 minutes. Cooking Time: 20 minutes. Serves 4.

2 tsp oil, preferably olive oil
½ cup chopped onions
3 cups vegetable stock, refer handy tip
Salt to taste
2 tsp cornflour mixed with ¼ cup water
1 tbsp chopped parsley for the garnish

For the potato balls
½ cup boiled, peeled and mashed potatoes

2 tbsp chopped parsley
½ tsp mustard (*rai*) powder
Salt to taste
¼ tsp freshly ground pepper

For the potato balls

1. Mix all the ingredients together and knead well.
2. Divide the mixture into 20 equal portions and shape them into small round balls. Keep aside.

How to proceed

1. Heat the oil in a non-stick pan, add the onions and sauté on a slow flame for 10 to 15 minutes till they turn golden brown in colour.
2. Add the vegetable stock and salt and bring to a boil.
3. Add the cornflour mixture and simmer for 5 minutes.
4. Just before serving, add the potato balls to the soup.
   Serve hot garnished with parsley.

Handy tip: To make vegetable stock, just add the vegetables like carrots, spring onions, capsicum and white pumpkin to a vesselful of water and simmer for about 20 minutes. Strain, use the liquid as stock and discard the vegetables.

Nutri Salad

Picture on page 19.

A medley of colourful veggies with a zesty apple-lemon juice-oregano dressing.

Preparation Time: 20 minutes. Cooking Time: Nil. Serves 4.

¼ cup shredded cabbage
¼ cup shredded red cabbage
¼ cup chopped tomatoes
½ cup thinly sliced carrots
½ cup thinly sliced cucumber
¼ cup thinly sliced red capsicum
¼ cup thinly sliced yellow capsicum
¼ cup thinly sliced green capsicum

To be mixed into a dressing
1 medium sized apple, grated with the skin
1 tbsp lemon juice

1 tsp sugar
½ tsp oregano
1 tbsp finely chopped raisins
⅛ tsp salt

Combine all the salad ingredients in a bowl, add the dressing to it and toss well. Serve immediately.

NUTRI SALAD : Recipe on page 17. →

Potato and Carrot Soup

Simple to taste and easy to cook. There are no spices used to help you prevent acidity, however herbs add the necessary taste and flavour.

Preparation Time: 10 minutes. Cooking Time: 20 minutes. Serves 4.

2 tsp butter
½ cup sliced onions
2½ cups potato cubes (preferably with the peel on)
1 tsp mixed dried herbs (oregano, thyme etc.)
Salt and freshly ground pepper to taste
2 tbsp grated carrot for the garnish

1. Heat the butter in a pressure cooker, add the onions and sauté for a while.
2. Add the potatoes and sauté for a few more minutes.
3. Add 4 cups of hot water and pressure cook for 3 whistles. Cool completely.
4. Put the cooked vegetables in a mixer and blend till smooth.
5. Add the herbs, salt and pepper and mix well and simmer for another 2 minutes. Serve hot garnished with the carrots.

Nourishing Lettuce Soup

This unusual yet delicious combination of lettuce and onions is sure to become a firm favourite, however avoid this soup if milk doesn't suit you.

Preparation Time: 15 minutes. Cooking Time: 20 minutes. Serves 6.

1½ tsp butter
1 cup chopped onions
6 cups chopped lettuce
2½ cups milk
2 tbsp plain flour (*maida*)
Salt and pepper to taste

1. Heat the butter in a vessel, add the onions and lettuce and sauté for a while.
2. Mix the milk and plain flour, add to the above mixture together with 2½ cups of water and cook for 10 minutes.
3. Cool to room temperature and blend in a mixer to a smooth purée.

4. Add the salt and pepper, mix well and simmer for 4 to 5 minutes.
   Serve hot.

Variation : **Nourishing Asparagus Soup**

Substitute the lettuce with 4 cups of chopped green asparagus in the above recipe.

Bean Sprouts Salad

Bean sprouts are full of vitamins and easy to digest. This easy to make salad which is healthy, colourful and crunchy can be enjoyed at any time of the day.

Preparation Time: 15 minutes. Cooking Time: Nil. Serves 4.

1 cup bean sprouts (washed and drained)
1 cup cucumber, peeled and cut into thin strips
½ cup carrots, peeled and cut into thin strips
½ cup chopped spring onions
½ cup apple cubes

To be mixed into a dressing
2 tbsp lemon juice
1 tbsp castor sugar
2 tbsp olive oil
½ tsp mustard (*rai / sarson*) powder
Salt and freshly ground pepper to taste

1. Combine the bean sprouts, cucumber, carrots and spring onions in a bowl and refrigerate to chill.
2. Just before serving, add the apples and dressing and toss well.
   Serve immediately.

Peas and Potato Salad

A mild, pleasantly flavoured dill sauce transforms this simple salad of peas and potatoes into an exotic delicacy.

Preparation Time: 15 minutes. Cooking Time: Nil. Serves 4.

2 cups boiled baby potatoes
1 cup boiled fresh green peas

To be mixed in a dressing
2 tbsp chopped dill leaves (*shepu / suva bhaji*)
½ cup hung curds (*dahi*)
1 tsp lemon juice
3 tbsp fresh cream
Salt and freshly ground pepper to taste

For the garnish
2 tbsp chopped fresh dill leaves (*shepu / suva bhaji*)

1. Combine the potatoes and peas in a serving bowl. Refrigerate to chill.
2. Just before serving, add the dressing and toss well.
   Serve immediately garnished with dill leaves.

Breakfasts and Snacks

Moong Sprouts Delight

A heapful of sprouts on khakhra make a great start for the day.

Preparation Time: 10 minutes. Cooking Time: 10 minutes. Serves 4.

2 tsp oil
1 tsp carom seeds (*ajwain*)
½ cup finely chopped onions
½ tsp chopped green chillies
1 cup *moong* (whole green gram) sprouts
Salt to taste
2 tbsp chopped coriander (*dhania*)
½ tsp lemon juice

For serving
Soya Sesame *Khakhra*, page 36

1. Heat the oil in a non-stick pan, add the carom seeds and fry till the seeds crackle.
2. Add the onions and green chillies and sauté till the onions turn translucent.
3. Add the sprouts and salt and sauté till the sprouts are cooked.
4. Add the coriander and lemon juice and toss well.
   Serve hot with Soya Sesame *Khakhra*.

Buckwheat Dhoklas

Enjoy this non-fermented, quick version of the famous Gujarati delicacy.

Preparation Time: 20 minutes. Cooking Time: 20 minutes. Serves 4.

½ cup buckwheat (*kutto or kutti no daro*)
¼ cup curds (*dahi*) mixed with ½ cup water
2 tbsp *ragi / nachni* (red millet) flour
1 tsp ginger-green chilli paste
Salt to taste
¼ tsp fruit salt
¼ tsp oil for greasing
1 tbsp chopped coriander (*dhania*) for the garnish

1. Grind the buckwheat coarsely. Wash and drain well.
2. Add the curds mixture and mix well.
3. Add the *ragi* flour, ginger-green chilli paste and salt to the mixture and mix well to make the *dhokla* batter.

4. Add the fruit salt to the batter and sprinkle a little water over it to enable bubbles to be formed.
5. Mix gently and pour the batter into a 200 mm. (8") diameter greased *thali.*
6. Steam for 15 to 20 minutes till the *dhoklas* are firm.
7. Cool slightly and cut into diamond-shaped pieces.

   Serve hot garnished with coriander.

Instant Jowar Uttapam

Picture on cover.

A variation to the rice and dal uttapam, made with jowar and urad dal which avoids the fermentation process and thus prevents acidity.

Preparation Time: 15 minutes. Cooking Time: 40 minutes. Makes 6 *uttapas*.
Soaking Time : Overnight.

¼ cup *jowar* (white millet)
1 tbsp *urad dal* (split black lentils)
1 tsp ginger-green chilli paste
½ tsp fruit salt
Salt to taste

Other ingredients
2 tsp oil for greasing and cooking
2 tbsp chopped tomatoes
1 tbsp chopped coriander (*dhania*)

1. Wash and soak the *jowar* and *urad dal* in enough water separately overnight.

2. Drain and blend them together in a mixer to a fine paste using little water.
3. Add the ginger-green chilli paste, fruit salt and salt to it and mix gently.
4. Pour a ladleful of this batter and pour it on a hot greased non-stick pan and spread it evenly to make a *uttapa* of 125 mm. (5") in diameter.
5. Sprinkle tomatoes and coriander on top and cook well on both sides using a little oil.

   Serve hot.

Crunchy Potato Pancakes

A wonderful recipe for a busy morning. Cook these pancakes as soon as you prepare the mixture, to prevent the potatoes from getting discoloured. To speed up your cooking, cook 2 to 3 pancakes at a time on a large non-stick pan.

Preparation Time: 10 minutes. Cooking Time: 25 minutes.
Makes 5 small pancakes.

½ cup grated raw potatoes
3 tbsp rice flour (*chawal ka atta*)
2 tbsp chopped coriander (*dhania*)
1 tsp roasted cumin seeds (*jeera*) powder
Salt to taste
1¼ tsp oil for cooking
3 tbsp chopped onions for the topping

1. Combine all the ingredients in a bowl, add 3 tbsp of water and mix well.
2. Divide the mixture into 5 equal portions.

3. Heat a non-stick pan and spread a portion of the mixture on the non-stick pan with the back of a spoon to make a circle of 75 mm. (3") diameter.
4. Cook on both sides using ¼ tsp oil till lightly cooked.
5. Sprinkle little onions on the pancake and cook on both sides till the onions are translucent.
6. Repeat with the remaining batter to make 4 more pancakes.

   Serve hot.

Nutritious Chilas

These yummy chilas are made using ragi, jowar and whole wheat flour.

Preparation Time: 4 minutes. Cooking Time: 10 minutes. Makes 8 *chilas*.

1/3 cup *jowar* flour (whole millet flour)
1/3 cup whole wheat flour (*gehun ka atta*)
1/3 cup *ragi* / *nachni* (red millet) flour
½ cup chopped onions
½ cup chopped tomatoes
2 tbsp chopped coriander (*dhania*)
1 green chilli, finely chopped
Salt to taste
2 tsp oil for greasing and cooking

1. Combine all the ingredients together in a bowl, add enough water to make a thin batter and divide into 8 equal parts.
2. Heat a non-stick pan and grease it lightly with oil.

3. Spread a portion of the batter to form a circle of 4 mm. thickness.
4. Cook on both sides till golden brown, using a little oil.
5. Repeat with the remaining batter to make 7 more *chilas*.
   Serve hot.

Soya Sesame Khakhra

Picture on facing page.

These crisp, oil-free khakhras will keep you going, right up till lunch. It abounds in all the nutrients except the fat, which is one of the culprits of acidity.

Preparation Time: 20 minutes. Cooking Time: 30 minutes. Makes 6 *khakhras*.

½ cup soya flour
¼ cup whole wheat flour *(gehun ka atta)*
1 tsp sesame seeds *(til)*, black and white
Salt to taste

1. Combine all the ingredients together in a bowl and knead into a firm dough using water as required. Keep aside for 10 to 15 minutes.
2. Divide the dough into 6 equal portions and roll out each portion into large thin circles of 150 mm. (6") in diameter.
3. Heat a non-stick pan and cook each circle over a low flame pressing from all sides with a cloth to make the *khakhras* crisp.
4. Cool and store in an air-tight container.

SOYA SESAME KHAKHRA : Recipe above. →

Veggie Wraps

A lavish breakfast ideal for Sunday menu.

Preparation Time: 25 minutes.   Cooking Time: 20 minutes.   Makes 4 wraps.

For the wraps
¾ cup whole wheat flour *(gehun ka atta)*
½ cup *jowar* (white millet) flour
1 tsp oil
Salt to taste
Whole wheat flour (*gehun ka atta*) for rolling

For the stuffing
1 tsp oil
1 cup grated cauliflower
½ cup grated carrots
½ cup shredded cabbage
½ cup boiled and grated potatoes
1 tbsp chopped coriander (*dhania*)

¼ tsp chilli powder
Salt to taste

For the wraps

1. Combine both the flours, oil and salt together in a bowl and knead to make a soft, smooth dough by adding enough hot water.
2. Knead the dough well and keep for ½ an hour. Knead again.
3. Divide the dough into 4 equal portions and roll out each portion into thin 150 mm. (6") diameter rounds with the help of a little flour.
4. Heat a non-stick pan and cook each *roti* till brown spots appear on both the sides. Keep aside.

For the stuffing

1. Heat the oil in a non-stick pan, add the cauliflower and carrots and sauté for 5 to 7 minutes or till it is cooked.
2. Add the cabbage, potatoes, coriander, chilli powder and salt and cook for 5 minutes.
3. Divide the stuffing into 4 equal portions and keep aside.

How to proceed

1. Place a *roti* on a clean flat surface, spread a portion of the stuffing evenly on it and roll it tightly to make a wrap.
2. Repeat with the remaining ingredients to make 3 more wraps.
   Serve hot.

Nachni Dosa

A newer version of dosa made with ragi.

Preparation Time: 15 minutes. Cooking Time: 30 minutes. Makes 6 *dosas*.
Soaking Time: Overnight.

1 cup *ragi / nachni* (red millet)
½ cup chopped onions
1 green chilli, chopped
1 tsp grated ginger
½ cup chopped coriander (*dhania*)
Salt to taste
1½ tsp oil for greasing and cooking

1. Wash and soak the *ragi* in enough water overnight.
2. Drain and grind to a paste in a mixer using a little water.
3. Add the onions, green chillies, ginger, coriander and salt and mix well.
4. Heat a non-stick pan and grease it lightly with a little oil.

5. Pour a spoonful of the batter to make a circle of 125 mm. (5") in diameter.
6. Cook on both sides till golden brown, using a little oil.
7. Repeat with the remaining batter to make 5 more *dosas*.
   Serve hot.

Variation : **Nachni Colocasia Dosa**

Substitute the coriander with ½ cup of finely chopped colocasia leaves (*arbi*) in the above recipe.

Onion Rawa Dosa

Another version of instant, non-fermented dosa made with semolina and onions.

Preparation Time: 10 minutes.   Cooking Time: 1 hour.
Makes 12 *rawa dosas.*

1 cup semolina *(rawa)*
1 cup rice flour (*chawal ka atta*)
¼ tsp soda bi-carb
2 tsp oil
½ tsp cumin seeds *(jeera)*
2 green chillies, chopped
A pinch asafoetida *(hing)*
A few curry leaves (*kadi patta*)
2 tbsp chopped fresh coconut
1½ tsp ghee for greasing and cooking
1½ cups sliced onions
Salt to taste

1. Combine the semolina, rice flour, soda bi-carb and salt and add enough water (approximately 4 cups) to make a very thin batter.
2. Add the onions, mix well and keep aside.
3. For the tempering, heat the oil in a small vessel, add the cumin seeds and fry until they crackle.
4. Add the green chillies, asafoetida and curry leaves and fry for a few seconds. Add this to the batter.
5. Add the coconut and mix well.
6. Heat a large non-stick *tava* (griddle) on a high flame and grease it lightly with a little ghee.
7. Pour ½ cup of the batter in a circular manner. Do not use a laddle to spread the batter, tilt and twirl the pan instead.
8. Drizzle a little ghee in the holes of the *dosa* and cook until crisp.
9. Fold into a triangular shape and serve hot.
10. Repeat with the remaining ingredients to make 11 more *dosas*.

Cabbage Jowar Muthias

These muthias make a great breakfast, when accompanied by a fruit or a fruit juice.

Preparation Time: 10 minutes. Cooking Time: 15 minutes. Serves 4.

For the *muthias*

1 cup grated cabbage
1 cup *jowar* (white millet) flour
5 tbsp curds *(dahi)*
1 tbsp chopped coriander (*dhania*)
1 tsp lemon juice
1 tsp ginger-green chilli paste
½ tsp turmeric powder *(haldi)*
A pinch soda bi-carb
1 tbsp sugar
Salt to taste

For the tempering

1 tsp oil
1 tsp cumin seeds *(jeera)*
¼ tsp asafoetida *(hing)*
3 to 4 curry leaves (*kadi patta*)

Other ingredients

¼ tsp oil for greasing
2 tbsp chopped coriander (*dhania*)
for the garnish

For the *muthias*

1. Combine all the ingredients together in a bowl and knead to make a soft dough using enough water.
2. Divide the dough into 3 equal parts and shape each portion into a cylindrical roll of approx. 125 mm. (5") in length.
3. Place the rolls on a greased steaming dish and steam over a medium flame for 10 to 12 minutes or till they are firm.
4. Remove, cool and cut into 25 mm (1") thick slices.

How to proceed

1. For the tempering, heat the oil in a non-stick pan, add the cumin seeds and fry till they crackle.
2. Add the asafoetida and curry leaves and fry for few more seconds.
3. Add the sliced *muthias* and sauté over a low flame till they are lightly browned. Serve hot garnished with coriander.

Rotis and Parathas

Nutritious Rotis

A combination of flours and vegetables to make these nourishing rotis. The lemon juice avoids the urge for spicy pickle as an accompaniment.

Preparation Time: 10 minutes. Cooking Time: 30 minutes. Makes 6 *rotis*.

¾ cup whole wheat flour *(gehun ka atta)*
¼ cup *besan* (Bengal gram flour)
¼ cup *jowar* (white millet) flour
¼ cup shredded cabbage
¼ cup finely chopped fenugreek leaves *(methi)*
½ tsp chopped green chillies
1 tbsp lemon juice
Salt to taste
Milk for binding the dough

1½ tsp ghee for cooking

1. Combine all the ingredients together in a bowl and knead into soft dough using enough milk.
2. Divide the dough into 6 equal portions.
3. Roll out each portion of the dough into a thick circle of 125 mm. (5") diameter.
4. Heat a non-stick pan and cook each *roti* till golden brown on both the sides using a little ghee.
   Serve hot.

Jowar Pyaz ki Roti

Jowar rotis flavoured with spring onions as a variation.

Preparation Time: 5 minutes. Cooking Time: 20 minutes. Makes 4 *rotis*.

1 cup *jowar* (white millet) flour
1 spring onion, finely chopped
1 green chilli, finely chopped
Salt to taste
1 tsp oil for cooking

1. Combine all the ingredients together in a bowl and knead into a soft dough, using warm water as required.
2. Cover and keep aside for 10 minutes.
3. Divide the dough into 4 equal portions.
4. Pat each portion on a dry flat surface using your palm to make a circle of 125 mm. (5") diameter.
5. Heat a non-stick pan and cook each *roti* using a little oil till it is lightly brown on both the sides.

   Serve hot.

Bajra Aloo Roti

Bajra is an alkali producing cereal; hence opt for this flour wherever possible. Potatoes besides adding flavour to this otherwise bland rotis also make them soft.

Preparation Time: 15 minutes. Cooking Time: 20 minutes. Makes 6 *rotis*.

1½ cups *bajra* (black millet) flour
¾ cup boiled and mashed potatoes
¼ cup finely chopped onions
3 to 4 tbsp chopped coriander *(dhania)*
1 tsp ginger-green chilli paste
¼ tsp freshly ground pepper powder
1 tsp dry mango powder (*amchur*)
½ tsp *garam masala* (optional)
Salt to taste
Bajra (black millet) flour for rolling
1 tbsp ghee for cooking

1. Combine all the ingredients together in a bowl and knead into a soft dough using hot water as required.
2. Divide the dough into 6 equal portions and roll out each portion into a 150 mm. (6") diameter circle.
3. Heat a non-stick pan and cook each *roti* using a little ghee, until both sides are golden brown.
   Serve hot.

Handy tip : Use a spoon to mix all the ingredients when adding the hot water and start kneading with your hands only after 5 minutes to prevent injury.

Minty Stuffed Parathas

Mint is known to relive acidity. Have fresh mint juice early in the morning or try these parathas to keep stomach acids at bay.

Preparation Time: 30 minutes. Cooking Time: 45 minutes. Makes 8 *parathas*.

For the dough
½ cup mint leaves (*phudina*)
1 tsp lemon juice
½ tsp cumin seeds (*jeera*)
1 tsp finely chopped green chillies
1 cup whole wheat flour (*gehun ka atta*)
½ tsp oil
Salt to taste

For the stuffing
½ cup chopped cabbage
Salt to taste
1 tsp oil
¼ cup mashed green peas
¼ cup chopped potatoes
¼ cup chopped onions
1 tsp lemon juice
½ tsp *garam masala*
1 tbsp chopped coriander (*dhania*)
½ tsp green chilli paste
½ tsp sugar

Other ingredients
2 tsp oil for cooking

For the dough

1. Combine the mint leaves, lemon juice, cumin seeds and green chillies along with ¼ cup of water and blend in a mixer to make a smooth paste.
2. Mix the prepared mint paste with the wheat flour, oil and salt and knead into a soft dough.
3. Divide the dough into 8 equal portions. Keep aside.

For the stuffing

1. Sprinkle salt over the cabbage and keep aside for 10 minutes. Thereafter, squeeze out the water from the cabbage using your hands.
2. Heat the oil in a pan and add the potatoes and green peas. Sprinkle a little water on top, cover and cook.
3. Add the cabbage and onions and cook for 1 minute.
4. Add the lemon juice, *garam masala*, coriander, green chilli paste, sugar and salt. Mix well.
5. Divide into 8 equal portions. Keep aside.

How to proceed

1. Roll each portion of the dough into a thin *chapati*.
2. Put one portion of the stuffing on each *chapati* and fold into half to make a *paratha*.
3. Cook each *paratha* on a non-stick pan using a little oil till both sides are golden brown in colour. Serve hot.

Suva Chawal Paratha

Picture on page 55.

Sweet variation of appas (rice bread) using suva bhaji. Knead the dough when hot otherwise it will harden on keeping. Not so very popular with many of you, suva bhaji is sweet to taste and is a rich source of vitamin A.

Preparation Time: 10 minutes.   Cooking Time: 15 minutes.   Makes 4 *parathas*.

½ cup chopped dill leaves *(shepu / suva bhaji)*
1½ cups rice flour (*chawal ka atta*)
Salt to taste
1 tsp finely chopped green chillies
Rice flour (*chawal ka atta*) for rolling
2 tsp oil for cooking

1. Combine the dill leaves and rice flour together in a bowl and mix well. Keep aside.
2. Put 1 cup of water to boil in a thick-bottom pan and add the salt and green chillies.
3. Add the dill leaves and rice flour mixture and stir for 2 minutes. Remove from the flame.

4. Cover it with a lid and leave aside for about 5 minutes.
5. Knead into soft dough using a little water if required.
6. Divide the dough into 4 equal portions.
7. Roll out each portion into a circle of 125 mm. (5") diameter, using a little rice flour.
8. Heat a non-stick pan and cook each *paratha*, using a little oil, till both sides are golden brown.
9. Repeat with the remaining portions to make 3 more *parathas*.
   Serve hot.

SUVA CHAWAL PARATHA : Recipe on page 53. →

Green Peas Paratha

A mildly spiced and satiating breakfast and main course that helps keep acidity at bay.

Preparation Time: 10 minutes. Cooking Time: 25 minutes. Makes 4 *parathas*.

For the dough

¾ cup whole wheat flour *(gehun ka atta)*
¼ cup soya flour
½ tsp salt
½ tsp ghee

For the stuffing

½ tbsp ghee
1 tsp cumin seeds *(jeera)*
½ tsp finely chopped green chillies
1 cup boiled green peas, mashed
Salt to taste

Other ingredients
Whole wheat flour *(gehun ka atta)* for rolling
1 tsp oil for cooking

For the dough
1. Sieve both the flours with the salt.
2. Combine the flours and ghee and knead to make a soft dough using enough water.
3. Divide the dough into 4 equal portions and keep aside.

For the stuffing
1. Heat the ghee in a pan and add the cumin seeds and fry till they crackle.
2. Add the green chillies and cook for 1 minute.
3. Add the mashed peas and salt and mix well.
4. Cool completely and divide the stuffing into 4 equal portions. Keep aside.

How to proceed
1. Roll out one portion of the dough into a circle of 75 mm. (3") diameter using flour for rolling.
2. Place one portion of the stuffing in the centre of the circle.
3. Bring together all the sides in the centre and seal tightly.

4. Roll out again into a circle of 150 mm. (6") in diameter, using flour for rolling.
5. Heat non-stick pan and cook each *paratha,* until both sides are golden brown using ¼ tsp of oil.
6. Repeat with the remaining dough and stuffing to make 3 more *parathas*.
   Serve hot.

Variation : **Pumpkin Paratha**

Substitute the green peas with 1 cup boiled and mashed pumpkin in the above recipe.

Subzis, Dals and Kadhis

Chawli Bhaji

This not-so-commonly used leafy vegetable cooked in minimal oil for you to enjoy it without worrying about acidity.

Preparation Time: 10 minutes.   Cooking Time: 15 minutes.   Serves 4.

4 cups chopped amaranth leaves (*chawli bhaji*)
A pinch turmeric powder (*haldi*)
Salt to taste
2 tsp oil
½ tsp mustard seeds (*rai / sarson*)
8 to 10 curry leaves (*kadi patta*)
2 whole dry red chillies, broken into pieces
1 tsp soaked *urad dal* (split black lentil)
A pinch asafoetida (*hing*)

1. Cook together the *chawli* leaves, turmeric powder and salt with 1 cup water over a medium flame, till the water dries out.
2. Remove from the flame and keep aside to cool.
3. When cool grind in a mixer into a fine paste. Keep aside.
4. Heat the oil in a non-stick pan and add the mustard seeds.
5. When they crackle, add the curry leaves, dry red chillies, *urad dal* and asafoetida and fry for a while.
6. Add the *chawli* paste and salt and bring to boil.

Serve hot.

Aloo Poshto

This traditional Bengali specialty is one of my favourite recipes and I recommend that you give this one a try. This recipe proves that poppy seeds and potatoes are a match made in heaven!

Preparation Time: 10 minutes. Cooking Time: 10 minutes. Serves 4.

2 tbsp poppy seeds (*khus-khus*)
2 tsp oil
2 whole dry red chillies, broken into pieces
½ tsp turmeric powder (*haldi*)
4 cups boiled potato cubes
Salt to taste

1. Heat a non-stick pan and dry roast the poppy seeds till they turn pink. Coarsely grind them in a mixer and keep aside.
2. Heat the oil in the same pan, add the red chillies, turmeric powder and ground poppy seeds and sauté for a minute.
3. Add the potatoes and salt and sauté for 2 to 3 more minutes.
   Serve hot.

Pyazwali Bhindi

Picture on page 1.

The usually fried ladies finger is here cooked in less oil and yet taste equally to suit the needs of people facing acidity due to oily food.

Preparation Time: 10 minutes.   Cooking Time: 20 minutes.   Serves 4.

2 tbsp oil
2 tsp cumin seeds *(jeera)*
1 tsp nigella seeds *(kalonji)*
1½ cups sliced onions
¼ tsp turmeric powder *(haldi)*
2 tsp ginger paste
1 tsp chopped green chillies
3 cups sliced ladies finger *(bhindi)*
Salt to taste
¾ cup thick fresh curds (*dahi*), whisked

1. Heat the oil in a non-stick pan, add the cumin seeds and nigella seeds.
2. When the seeds crackle, add the onions, turmeric powder, ginger paste and green chillies and cook till the onions are tender. Sprinkle little water if the mixture becomes dry.
3. Add the *bhindi* and salt and cook over a medium flame till the *bhindi* is tender.
4. Add the whisked curds and cook till the curds dry out.

   Serve hot with *parathas* or *rotis*.

Handy tips :

1. *Bhindi* tends to get sticky while cooking. Do not cover the pan while cooking and the stickiness will dry out without the presence of steam.
2. Cook the *bhindi* over a slow flame for best results.

Avial

Picture on facing page.

This South Indian curry has an unusual combination of vegetables, which makes the dish particularly flavourful. An ideal companion for a bowl of steaming hot rice.

Preparation Time: 10 minutes.   Cooking Time: 20 minutes.   Serves 4.

½ cup drumsticks, cut into 25 mm. (1") pieces
½ cup French beans, cut into 25 mm. (1") pieces
½ cup cauliflower florets
½ cup potato cubes
½ cup fresh green peas
½ cup brinjal (*baingan* / eggplant) cubes
Salt to taste
¼ cup fresh curds (*dahi*), whisked
1 tsp oil

AVIAL : Recipe above. →

For the paste

½ cup grated fresh coconut
½ tsp cumin seeds *(jeera)*
1 small green chilli, roughly chopped
¼ tsp turmeric powder *(haldi)*

For the paste

Blend all the ingredients with ¼ cup of water to a smooth paste. Keep aside.

How to proceed

1. Combine the drumsticks along with ¼ cup of water in a non-stick pan, cover and cook till the drumsticks are half done.
2. Add the remaining vegetables and salt and mix well. Cover and cook till the vegetables are tender.
3. Add the prepared paste, curds and 1 cup of water and bring to boil. Simmer for 5 to 6 minutes.
4. Add the oil and simmer for half a minute.
   Serve hot.

Subz Bahar

This Hyderabadi korma is mildly spiced and has it own distinct flavour. A variety of vegetables used here, makes this korma very colourful and also tasty.

Preparation Time: 10 minutes. Cooking Time: 20 minutes. Serves 4.

2 tsp oil
½ tsp cumin seeds *(jeera)*
2 medium onions, puréed
2 cloves *(laung / lavang)*
25 mm. (1") stick cinnamon *(dalchini)*
1 cardamom *(elaichi)*
1 tsp ginger-garlic paste
½ tsp green chilli paste
¼ cup cauliflower, cut into small florets
¼ cup French beans, cut into 25 mm (1") pieces
¼ cup carrot cubes
¼ cup fresh green peas

½ cup capsicum cubes
¼ cup baby corn, cut into slices
1 cup milk
3 tbsp cream
½ tsp *garam masala*
Salt to taste
1 tbsp chopped coriander *(dhania)* for the garnish

1. Heat the oil in a non-stick pan and add the cumin seeds.
2. When they crackle, add the onion purée, cloves, cinnamon, cardamom, ginger-garlic paste and green chilli paste and sauté for 5 to 7 minutes, while stirring continuously.
3. Add the cauliflower, French beans, carrots, green peas, capsicum, baby corn, ½ cup of milk and ¼ cup of water. Cover and cook over a slow flame till the vegetables are tender.
4. Add the remaining milk, cream, *garam masala* and salt and simmer for another 3 to 4 minutes.

   Serve hot garnished with coriander.

Kaddu ka Bharta

Pumpkin, a vegetable that is not appreciated by many. However knowing that it is an alkali producing food, will surely win its fans facing acidity problems.

Preparation time: 5 minutes.   Cooking time: 20 minutes.   Serves 4.

2 tsp oil
1 tsp cumin seeds *(jeera)*
1 tsp fennel seeds *(saunf)*
1 tsp nigella seeds *(kalonji)*
A pinch fenugreek *(methi)* seeds
½ cup finely chopped onions
4 cups chopped red pumpkin *(kaddu)*
A pinch asafoetida *(hing)*
½ tsp turmeric powder *(haldi)*
¼ tsp chilli powder
Salt to taste
2 tsp dry mango powder *(amchur)*

1. Heat the oil in a pressure cooker and add the cumin seeds, fennel seeds, nigella seeds and fenugreek seeds.
2. When the seeds crackle, add the onions and sauté till they turn translucent.
3. Add the pumpkin, asafoetida, turmeric powder, chilli powder and salt with ½ cup of water and pressure cook for 2 whistles so that the pumpkin becomes mushy.
4. Add the dry mango powder and salt and mix well.
   Serve hot.

Hariyali Dal

Hariyali means 'green', so is this dal that is made by adding a combination of green leafy vegetables like chawli, methi and coriander.

Preparation Time: 10 minutes. Cooking Time: 20 minutes. Serves 4.

½ cup *masoor dal* (split red lentils)
2 tsp oil
1 tsp cumin seeds (*jeera*)
¼ cup chopped onions
1½ cups greens (*chawli bhaji*, fenugreek leaves and coriander)
1 tsp dry mango powder (*amchur*)
½ cup chopped tomatoes
½ tsp turmeric powder *(haldi)*
Salt to taste

To be ground into a paste
3 cloves garlic
2 green chillies

25 mm. (½") piece ginger

1. Combine the *dal* along with 2 cups of water and pressure cook for 3 whistles. Keep aside.
2. Heat the oil in a non-stick pan, add the cumin seeds and onions and sauté for 2 minutes.
3. Add the cooked *dal,* greens, dry mango powder, tomatoes, turmeric powder, the ground paste, ½ cup of water and salt and cook for a 5 to 7 minutes.
   Serve hot.

Mixed Dal

Picture on page 75.

Confused what should you make for lunch, don't worry! This delicious dal combined with Suva Chawal Paratha, page 53, makes a complete meal.

Preparation Time: 15 minutes. Cooking Time: 25 minutes. Serves 4.

2 tbsp yellow *moong dal* (split yellow gram)
1 tbsp *masoor dal* (split red lentil)
1 tbsp *urad dal* (split red lentil)
Salt to taste
½ tsp turmeric powder *(haldi)*
1 tbsp butter
½ tsp cumin seeds *(jeera)*
¼ cup chopped onions
1 tsp chopped green chillies
1 tsp chopped ginger
½ cup chopped tomatoes
2 tbsp chopped coriander *(dhania)*

1. Combine all the 3 *dals* along with 1 cup of water, salt and turmeric powder and pressure cook for 2 whistles. Keep aside.
2. Heat the butter in a non-stick pan and add the cumin seeds.
3. When they crackle, add the onions, green chillies and ginger and sauté for 2 minutes.
4. Add the tomatoes, coriander, cooked *dals* and add ½ cup water and cook for 5 minutes.

   Serve hot.

MIXED DAL : Recipe on page 73. →

Suva Moong Dal

Dill, another leafy vegetable that's alkaline in nature thereby making this dal a "go for it" dish for those who complain about acidity.

Preparation Time: 10 minutes. Cooking Time: 25 minutes. Serves 4.

½ cup yellow *moong dal* (split yellow gram)
¼ tsp turmeric powder *(haldi)*
Salt to taste
1 tbsp oil
½ tsp cumin seeds *(jeera)*
2 to 3 curry leaves *(kadi patta)*
1 tsp chopped garlic
½ tsp chopped green chillies
½ cup finely chopped onions
2 tbsp chopped dill leaves *(shepu / suva bhaji)*

1. Clean, wash and soak the *dal* in water for about 30 minutes. Drain.

2. Add the turmeric powder, salt and 2 cups of water and pressure cook for 2 whistles or till the *dal* is done.
3. Whisk well to mash the *dal* and keep aside.
4. Heat oil in a non-stick pan and add the cumin seeds.
5. When they crackle, add the curry leaves, garlic, green chillies and onions and sauté till the onions turn translucent.
6. Add the cooked *dal*, dill leaves, 1 cup of water and bring to a boil.
7. Simmer for 10 minutes and serve hot.

Sindhi Kadhi

A bowlful of this kadhi along with steaming hot rice is just right for a wholesome Sunday lunch.

Preparation Time: 20 minutes. Cooking Time: 20 minutes. Serves 4.

¼ cup cluster beans *(gavarfali)*
½ cup potato cubes
¼ cup carrots cubes
2 tsp oil
½ tsp cumin seeds *(jeera)*
½ tsp fenugreek *(methi)* seeds
¼ tsp asafoetida *(hing)*
¼ cup *besan* (Bengal gram flour)
½ tsp chopped green chillies
1 tsp grated ginger
4 to 6 curry leaves (*kadi patta*)
¼ tsp turmeric powder *(haldi)*
½ tsp chilli powder

1 to 2 tbsp tamarind *(imli)* pulp
¼ cup *bhindi* (ladies finger), slit into 2 vertically
Salt to taste

1. Boil 2 cups of water in a pan, add the cluster beans, potatoes and carrots and cook till they are tender. Keep aside, retaining the water.
2. Heat the oil in a non-stick pan and add the cumin seeds and fenugreek seeds.
3. When they crackle add the asafoetida and fry for a few seconds.
4. Add the *besan* and sauté for 4 to 5 minutes over a medium flame till it is golden brown.
5. Add 4 cups of water and bring to boil.
6. Add the green chillies, ginger, curry leaves, turmeric powder, chilli powder, tamarind pulp, ladies finger, all the cooked vegetables and salt.
7. Bring to boil and simmer till the ladies finger is cooked.
   Serve hot.

Methi Koftas in Kadhi

Easy to make and yummy to taste even with the addition of non-fried koftas is just enough to describe this kadhi.

Preparation Time: 20 minutes. Cooking Time: 30 minutes. Serves 4.

For the *methi koftas*
1 cup finely chopped fenugreek (*methi*) leaves
Salt to taste
2 tbsp whole wheat flour (*gehun ka atta*)
2 tbsp *bajra* (black millet) flour
1 tbsp semolina (*rawa*)
½ tsp ginger-green chilli paste
A pinch of turmeric powder (*haldi*)
½ tsp lemon juice
½ tsp sugar
A pinch soda bi-carb

For the *kadhi*

1 cup fresh curds (*dahi*), whisked
2 tbsp *besan* (Bengal gram flour)
1 tsp oil
1 tsp cumin seeds (*jeera*)
A pinch asafoetida (*hing*)
5 curry leaves (*kadi patta*)
⅓ cup sliced onions
2 cloves garlic, finely chopped
¼ tsp turmeric powder (*haldi*)
Salt to taste

For the *methi koftas*

1. Add the salt to the *methi* leaves and keep aside for 5 minutes.
2. Squeeze the *methi* to drain out all the water and place it in a bowl.
3. Add all the remaining ingredients and a little more salt and knead to a soft dough adding a little water if required.
4. Apply a little water on your hand and shape the dough into small *koftas*.
5. Steam in a steamer till done. Keep aside.

For the *kadhi*

1. Combine the curds and *besan* in a bowl, add 1½ cups of water and whisk well till no lumps remain. Keep aside.
2. Heat the oil in a pan and add the cumin seeds.
3. When they crackle, add the asafoetida, curry leaves, onions and garlic and sauté for 4 to 5 minutes.
4. Add the curds-*besan* mixture, turmeric powder and salt and bring to boil over a slow flame. Keep aside.

How to proceed

1. Just before serving, add the *methi koftas* to the hot *kadhi*.
2. Bring to boil and serve hot.

Aloo Gobhi ka Pulao

Picture on page 85.

Aloo and gobhi, an age-old combination that is one of my favourites too. I made a pulao using it just for fun and it turned out to be an invention in itself.

Preparation Time: 10 minutes. Cooking Time: 20 minutes. Serves 4.

2 cups long grained rice (*basmati*)
2 tsp oil
2 bayleaves *(tejpatta)*
25 mm. (1") cinnamon *(dalchini)*
½ tsp turmeric powder *(haldi)*
¼ tsp dry ginger powder *(soonth)*
½ tsp chilli powder
1 cup potato cubes

1 cup cauliflower florets
Salt to taste
½ tsp *garam masala*
A few mint sprigs *(phudina),* for the garnish

1. Clean, wash and soak the rice for approx. 15 minutes. Drain and keep aside.
2. Heat the oil in a pressure cooker and add the bayleaves and cinnamon and fry for few seconds.
3. Add the turmeric powder, dry ginger powder, chilli powder, potatoes and cauliflower and sauté for 2 minutes.
4. Add the rice and sauté for 2 more minutes.
5. Add 3 cups of hot water and salt and pressure cook for 2 whistles.
6. Allow the steam to escape before opening the lid.
7. Add the *garam masala* and mix gently.
   Serve hot garnished with mint sprigs.

ALOO GOBHI KA PULAO : Recipe on page 83. →

Cucumber Curd Rice

Cucumber is considered one of the best vegetables for combating acidity. When combined with curds and carrots it does wonders for your taste buds and stomach.

Preparation Time: 10 minutes. Cooking Time: 15 minutes. Serves 4.

To be mixed together for the rice mixture

¾ cup cooked rice, cooled and mashed slightly
1½ cup fresh curds *(dahi)*
1 cup cucumber, washed and chopped
1 cup grated carrots
¼ cup chopped coriander *(dhania)*
Salt to taste
½ cup water

For the tempering

1 tsp oil
1 tsp cumin seeds *(jeera)*
1 tbsp *urad dal* (split black lentils)
1 green chilli, slit
½ tsp asafoetida *(hing)*
4 to 6 curry leaves (*kadi patta*)

For the tempering

1. Heat the oil in a non-stick pan and add the cumin seeds.
2. When they crackle, add the *urad dal*, green chilli, asafoetida, curry leaves and sauté for 1 minute.

How to proceed

1. Pour the tempering over the rice mixture and mix well.
2. Refrigerate for a few hours.
   Serve chilled.

Green Peas and Methi Pulao

If plain rice give you acidity, try this pulao with a difference.

Preparation Time: 10 minutes. Cooking Time: 10 minutes. Serves 4.

2 tsp oil
1¼ cups long grained rice (*basmati*)
2 cups chopped fenugreek leaves (*methi*)
½ cup green peas
1½ tsp ginger-green chilli paste
Salt to taste
2 tbsp chopped coriander (*dhania)*
for the garnish

1. Clean, wash and soak the rice for about 10 minutes. Drain and keep aside.
2. Blanch the fenugreek leaves in hot water for 2 minutes. Keep aside.
3. Heat the oil in a pressure cooker, add the rice and sauté for few seconds.
4. Add the fenugreek leaves, peas, ginger-green chilli paste, salt and 2½ cups of hot water and pressure cook for 2 whistles.
5. Allow the steam to escape before opening the lid. Separate each grain of rice lightly with fork.

   Serve hot garnished with coriander.

Soyabean and Vegetable Pulao

Soyabean is a versatile food not just because of it health benefits but also for its effect on stomach once it is consumed. It produces alkali in the stomach thereby making its place in the list of alkaline foods.

Preparation Time: 5 minutes. Cooking Time: 15 minutes. Serves 4.
Soaking Time: 15 minutes.

½ cup soya granules
1 tsp oil
½ tsp cumin seeds *(jeera)*
1 small stick cinnamon *(dalchini)*
1 green cardamom *(elaichi)*
A pinch asafoetida *(hing)*
½ cup chopped onions
½ cup peeled and chopped carrots
½ cup green peas
1½ cups long grained rice (*basmati*), washed and drained
¼ tsp chilli powder

¼ tsp turmeric powder *(haldi)*
1 tsp coriander-cumin seeds *(dhania-jeera)* powder
Salt to taste
¼ cup chopped coriander *(dhania)* for the garnish

1. Soak the soya granules in 1 cup of hot water for 15 to 20 minutes. Drain and keep aside.
2. Heat the oil in a pressure cooker and add the cumin seeds, cinnamon and cardamom.
3. When the cumin seeds crackle, add the asafoetida and onions and sauté for 2 to 3 minutes.
4. Add the carrots, green peas, rice and soya granules and sauté for another 2 minutes.
5. Add the chilli powder, turmeric powder, coriander-cumin seeds powder and salt and mix well.
6. Add 4 cups of hot water and pressure cook for 2 whistles.
   Served hot garnished with the coriander.

Handy tip : If the soya granules are hard to find, use 8 to 10 soya nuggets instead. Boil them first and then chop them finely.

Wholesome Khichdi

Simple to make, this khichdi is balanced in itself as is made with rice, dal, and lots of vegetables. Relish it with hot kadhi or plain fresh curds.

Preparation Time: 10 minutes.   Cooking Time: 25 minutes.   Serves 4.

½ cup rice
¾ cup yellow *moong dal* (split yellow gram)
½ tbsp ghee
1 tsp cumin seeds *(jeera)*
½ tsp asafoetida *(hing)*
2-3 peppercorns
1 bayleaf *(tejpatta)*
2 cloves *(laung / lavang)*
1 cup grated bottle gourd *(doodhi / lauki)*
1 cup grated carrots
½ tsp turmeric powder *(haldi)*
Salt to taste

1. Clean and wash the rice and *moong dal* together. Drain and keep aside.
2. Heat the ghee in a pressure cooker and add the cumin seeds.
3. When they crackle, add the asafoetida, peppercorns, bayleaf and cloves.
4. Add the bottle gourd and carrots and sauté for a few seconds.
5. Add the rice, *moong dal*, turmeric powder, salt and 4½ cups of hot water and pressure cook for 2 whistles.
6. When done, whisk the *khichdi* to combine the rice and *dal* together.
   Serve hot.

Bajra Khichdi

Picture on page 2.

Stuffed to the core with iron health, this khichdi is a treat for elders and the children in the family!

Preparation Time: 10 minutes. Cooking Time: 15 minutes. Serves 4.

1/3 cup whole *bajra* (black millet)
3 tbsp yellow *moong dal* (split yellow gram)
Salt to taste
1 tbsp ghee
1 tsp cumin seeds (*jeera*)
½ tsp asafoetida (*hing*)

1. Grind the *bajra* to a coarse powder in a blender.
2. Combine the *bajra* powder and *moong dal* with salt and 2½ cups of hot water and pressure cook for 3 whistles.
3. Heat the ghee in a pan and add the cumin seeds and asafoetida.
4. When they crackle, pour over the cooked *khichdi* and mix well.
   Serve hot.

Apple Cinnamon Milkshake

"An apple a day keeps the doctor away" also proves true for acidity when whipped up as a milkshake, as chilled milk is known to overcome acidity for some people.

Preparation Time: 10 minutes. Cooking Time: Nil. Makes 4 glasses.

1½ cups peeled and chopped apples
2 tbsp sugar
2 cups chilled milk
1 tsp cinnamon *(dalchini)* powder
Crushed ice to serve

1. Blend the apple and sugar in a blender to a smooth purée using a little milk.
2. Add the cinnamon powder and milk and blend again.
3. Pour into 4 individual glasses and top with ice-cubes.
   Serve immediately.

Date and Banana Shake

Make the most use of these high alkaline bananas by whipping a shake early in the morning.

Preparation Time: 15 minutes. Cooking Time: 5 minutes. Makes 2 glasses.

1½ cups milk
¼ cup dates *(khajur)*, deseeded
1 banana
1 tsp sugar (optional)
4 to 6 ice-cubes

1. Heat the milk in a pan and soak the dates in it for 10 to 15 minutes till they soften keep aside to cool.
2. Combine the soaked dates, milk, banana and sugar with ice-cubes in a mixer and blend till smooth.
3. Pour into 2 individual glasses and serve immediately.

Papaya Mango Smoothie

Papaya and mango both are said to be alkaline by nature and hence good for acidity. Do remember to try this variation when mango is in season.

Preparation Time: a few minutes. Cooking Time: Nil. Makes 2 glasses.

1 cup chopped papaya
1 cup fresh chopped mangoes
1 tbsp sugar (optional)
1 tbsp lemon juice (optional)
Crushed ice to serve

1. Combine all the ingredients except the ice in the mixer and blend till smooth.
2. Add some crushed ice into 2 individual glasses and pour the smoothie over it. Serve immediately.

Strawberry Chickoo Shake

This is one of my favourite breakfast shakes. When I am in hurry, I simply gulp it down to prevent acidity.

Preparation Time: 5 minutes. Cooking Time: Nil. Makes 2 glasses.

½ cup chopped ripe strawberries
½ cup peeled and chopped chickoo
1 cup chilled milk

1. Combine all the ingredients in a mixer and blend till smooth.
2. Pour into 2 individual glasses.
   Serve chilled.

Handy tip : Add 1 tsp of sugar to the shake if the fruits are not well ripe.

Kokum Sherbet

Picture on backcover.

This chilled sherbet is a healthy substitute for carbonated or caffienated drinks and is a great acidity reliever.

Preparation Time: 15 minutes. Cooking Time: 5 minutes.
Makes 12 to 15 glasses.

½ cup semi-dried *kokum*
½ cup sugar
1 tsp roasted cumin seeds *(jeera)* powder
½ tsp black salt *(sanchal)*
Ice-cubes to serve

1. Soak the *kokum* in 1 cup of water for 2 to 3 hours. Drain and preserve the *kokum* water.
2. Blend in a mixer using ½ cup of the preserved *kokum* water, to obtain a smooth purée.

3. Combine the sugar with the remaining kokum water and heat the mixture in a pan to obtain a 1 string consistency sugar syrup. Keep aside to cool.
4. Add the puréed *kokum*, roasted cumin seeds powder and black salt and mix well.
5. Strain and pour into a sterilized air-tight bottle.
6. When serving, add 1 tbsp of this syrup into a tall glass along with 3 to 4 ice-cubes and top with cold water.
   Stir and serve immediately.

Melon and Papaya Tango

This snazzy orange coloured-carbohydrate rich juice is a fulfilling breakfast idea. The papaya being alkaline by nature prevents acidity and the lemon juice makes it more interesting by imparting its flavourful touch.

Preparation Time: 5 minutes. Cooking Time: Nil. Makes 2 glasses.

¾ cup papaya (peeled), deseeded and cut into pieces
1 cup peeled muskmelon *(kharbooja)*, cut into pieces
½ tsp lemon juice
Crushed ice to serve

1. Blend all the ingredients in a mixer using little water till smooth.
2. Strain the juice using a strainer or a muslin cloth.
3. Add the lemon juice and mix well.
4. Add some crushed ice in 2 individual glasses and pour the juice over it. Serve immediately.

Pineapple Magic

Here's a contrasting flavour of pineapple and ginger along with coriander to prevent acidity.

Preparation Time: 5 minutes.   Cooking Time: Nil.   Makes 2 glasses.

1½ cups chopped pineapple
3 tbsp coriander (*dhania*) sprigs with the leaves, roughly chopped
12 mm. (½") piece ginger
Crushed ice to serve

1. Blend all the ingredients in a mixer using little water till smooth.
2. Strain the juice using a strainer or a muslin cloth.
3. Add some crushed ice in 2 individual glasses and pour the juice over it. Serve immediately.

Rainbow Cocktail

Luscious oranges when blended with zesty sweet lime and black grapes make a favourite anytime drink. Serve it with a hint of black salt for that added zing!

Preparation Time: 5 minutes. Cooking Time: Nil. Makes 2 glasses.

2 big oranges (peeled), separated into segments
1 medium sized sweet lime (peeled), separated into segments
¼ cup black grapes
1 tbsp lemon juice
½ tsp black salt (*sanchal*) (optional)
Crushed ice to serve

1. Blend all the ingredients in a mixer using little water till smooth.
2. Strain the juice using a strainer or a muslin cloth.
3. Add the lemon juice and black salt and mix well.
4. Add some crushed ice in 2 individual glasses and pour the juice over it. Serve immediately.

Total Health Series by Tarla Dalal

The Total Health series is a range of cookbooks specially designed and carefully researched by a team of qualified nutritionists. These books are an action-oriented guide for good health and wellness to suit the nutritional needs for different age groups, be it an expectant mum, a baby, an individual who has a medical problem or aims to lose weight. These books will help you and your family stay in fine fettle. They have opened new vistas in the field of cooking while providing you with healthy guidelines for adding verve and vitality to your life. Some of the titles in this series are:

Low Calorie Healthy Cooking

Pregnancy Cook Book

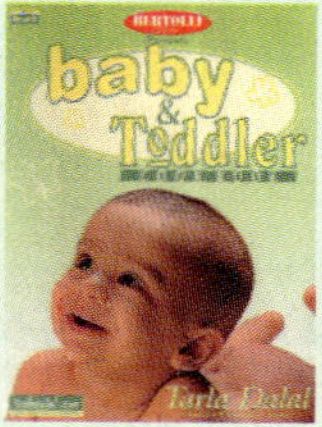

Baby & Toddler Cook Book

Healthy Heart Cook Book

Cooking with 1 Teaspoon of Oil

Delicious Diabetic Recipes